The Biography Of Zac Efron

Zac Efron and his Resilient Quest for Survival

By

Winston Hayes

Table of Contents

Childhood and Background

On October 18, 1987, Zachary David Alexander Efron, better known as Zac Efron, emerged from the magnificent surroundings of San Luis Obispo, California. His father, David Efron, an electrical engineer, and mother, Starla Baskett, an administrative assistant, created a loving atmosphere for the young talent to blossom. Growing up in Arroyo Grande, California, Efron's childhood was "normal," according to him, but it was defined by a deep interest in entertainment.

Dylan, a younger brother, and Olivia, a younger paternal half-sister, were part of the Efron family dynamics. Zac's adventure began within the confines of this supportive familial cocoon, establishing the groundwork for a fantastic career that would eventually see him climb to prominence in the entertainment business.

Zac's surname, Efron, carries a hint of lineage, deriving from Hebrew roots. His paternal grandfather's Jewish ancestry provides a layer of cultural complexity to his background, which would become important as he navigated his personal and professional life.

Despite his Jewish ancestry, Efron views his upbringing as agnostic. Religion did not play a significant role in his upbringing, yet echoes of cultural diversity persist in the background of his identity. It's a thread that runs through his life's fabric, shaping his perspective and providing depth to his path.

Zac's lively attitude and early hints of the entertainer within began to radiate through the hallways of Arroyo Grande High School. After graduating in 2006, he faced a decision between furthering his study at the University of Southern California and entering the volatile world of entertainment. While admitted to USC, Efron chose to forego regular academics in order to pursue the unorthodox route that attracted him.

The stage's attraction and footlights beckoned to Efron. His first forays into the entertainment industry included appearances at The Great American Melodrama and Vaudeville, where his flair for drama attracted an appreciative audience. During this time, he started taking singing lessons, establishing the groundwork for a skill that would later become an important aspect of his career.

Zac moved to Los Angeles after being recommended by his drama teacher, Robyn Metchik, and was signed by the Creative Artists Agency. This was the start of a career that would quickly propel him to international stardom. Efron's early years in show business were marked by effort, determination, and an unrelenting commitment to his trade.

As we peel back the layers of Zac Efron's childhood, it becomes clear that his path from the sunlit streets of Arroyo Grande to the bustling avenues of Hollywood was the product of a combination of skill, ambition, and a dash of destiny.

A Career Overview of Zac Efron

Zac Efron's career is a tapestry woven with different threads of brilliance, variety, and a willingness to venture beyond the boundaries of expectation. In the early 2000s, he made his debut in the entertainment industry as a guest star on television shows such as Firefly, ER, and The Guardian. However, it wasn't until 2004 that he earned a recurring role in the WB series Summerland, signalling the start of a more significant presence on the screen.

In 2006, he had his debut with the teen musical television picture High School Musical. Efron won the hearts of a global audience as Troy Bolton, a high school basketball player torn between sports and the school musical. The success of the film not only launched him into the spotlight, but also highlighted his musical abilities. Despite the fact that the role was written for a tenor, Efron, a baritone, rose to the occasion, establishing a precedent for his future musical endeavours.

Following the success of High School Musical, Efron moved into the musical comedy genre with Hairspray (2007), demonstrating his ability to fluidly switch between roles. His dedication to his art shined through even when faced with logistical hurdles while filming Hairspray alongside the High School Musical musical tour.

High School Musical 2 (2007) and High School Musical 3: Senior Year (2008) continued Efron's journey, all of which contributed to the franchise's massive popularity. The latter was an important milestone because it was the first picture in the series to be released theatrically, cementing Efron's prominence as a box office draw.

Efron displayed a desire to break free from the restrictions of his "Disney pretty boy" image as he negotiated the post-High School Musical world. In the financially successful comedy 17 Again (2009), he played a 37-year-old guy converted into his 17-year-old self.

In the years since, Efron has played a variety of roles. He demonstrated a variety that extended beyond the musical genre, from the period drama Me and Orson Welles (2008) to the love drama The Lucky One (2012). Despite mixed reviews, Efron continued to experiment with his selections, blending financial success with critical appreciation.

The hilarious success of Neighbours (2014) represented a watershed moment in his career, removing the last vestiges of his Disney persona and establishing him as a capable performer in adult comedy. The success of the film paved the way for other popular comedies, such as Dirty Grandpa (2016) and Neighbours 2: Sorority Rising (2016), demonstrating Efron's ability to negotiate varied comedic environments.

In 2017, Efron starred in Baywatch, a film remake of the classic television series, and appeared in The Disaster Artist and The Greatest Showman as a supporting actor. These projects highlighted his dedication to experimenting with many genres and cemented his place as a leading man in Hollywood.

In the years since, Efron has taken on darker parts, most notably as Ted Bundy in Extremely Wicked, Shockingly Evil, and Vile (2019). This divergence from his previous roles demonstrated his willingness to stretch himself and play complex characters.

Efron's accomplishments expanded beyond the silver screen to hosting. His Daytime Emmy Award in 2021 for anchoring the Netflix travel show Down to Earth with Zac Efron adds a new layer to his already diverse career.

As we delve deeper into Zac Efron's career, it becomes clear that it is more than a series of films; it is a story of transformation, resilience, and a never-ending search for artistic progress. Zac Efron's career portrays a vision of an artist constantly pushing limits and confounding expectations, from the bright lights of High School Musical to the subtle performances in subsequent years.

Arroyo Grande to Hollywood Lights

Zac Efron's journey from the tranquil town of Arroyo Grande to the brilliant lights of Hollywood is a riveting story that reveals the actor's core layers. This chapter dives into his formative influences and family dynamics, examining the early hints of a performance passion that would eventually characterise his career.

Family and Childhood Influences

Zachary David Alexander Efron was born on October 18, 1987, in San Luis Obispo, California, as Zachary David Alexander Efron. He spent his early years in Arroyo Grande. His parents, David Efron, an electrical engineer at Diablo Canyon Power Plant, and Starla Baskett, an administrative assistant at the same plant, laid a solid basis for his upbringing. With a younger brother, Dylan, and a younger paternal half-sister, Olivia, Efron had what he calls a "normal childhood" in a middle-class household.

While the Efrons were not overtly artistic, they were supportive of Zac's pursuits. His early exposure to the performing arts began within the context of familial connections. Efron had a natural curiosity and aptitude for entertaining as a child, frequently displaying his affinity for mimicking and dramatic emotions during family gatherings. Recognising this spark, his parents pushed him to pursue his creative interests.

With its Hebrew origins, Efron's surname lends another depth to his identity. With a Jewish paternal grandfather, Efron identifies as Jewish, despite his upbringing being mainly agnostic and devoid of religious customs. This eclectic tapestry of heritage is quietly woven into the fabric of his identity, contributing to Zac Efron's one-of-a-kind mosaic.

Efron's drive for perfection was evident in his early academic studies. He was the type of student who would "flip out" if he got a "B" rather than a "A." The academic context, on the other hand, revealed his sense of humour, as he took on the position of class clown. This dual personality, a mix of diligence and a humorous energy, would eventually serve him well on stage and television.

Early education and a strong desire to perform

During Efron's high school years, the voyage from Arroyo Grande to the world's entertainment centre began to take form. After graduating from Arroyo Grande High School in 2006, Efron found himself at the intersection between formal education and a growing interest in the performing arts. He was accepted to the University of Southern California but chose not to attend, instead choosing a new path that would lead him to the world of acting.

Efron also attended the Pacific Conservatory of the Performing Arts, a theatre group affiliated with Allan Hancock College, during these formative years. During this time, he immersed himself in the realm of stage performances, honing his craft and laying the groundwork for a career in the entertainment industry. His participation in shows such as "Gipsy," "Little Shop of Horrors," and "The Music Man" displayed not just his acting abilities but also his developing singing prowess.

A suggestion from his theatre teacher, Robyn Metchik, who also happened to be the mother of actor Aaron Michael Metchik, was the spark for Efron's transfer from local performances to the grandeur of Hollywood. This link led to Efron being signed by the Creative Artists Agency, a watershed moment that paved the stage for his entrée into the larger entertainment industry.

The chapter unfolds not just as a chronicle of Efron's personal journey, but also as a monument to the role of family support, cultural influences, and a never-ending quest of passion in defining the fate of a growing artist. Little did the ambitious actor from Arroyo Grande know that these early chapters would pave the way for a Hollywood saga that would transcend the silver screen, making him a household celebrity and a symbol of young exuberance in the entertainment industry.

Getting a Job in Hollywood

Zac Efron's journey into Hollywood is a captivating story of ambition, talent, and tenacity. Efron's early infatuation with the world of entertainment as a young boy growing up in Arroyo Grande, California, sparked a passion that would soon catapult him into the spotlight.

Theatrical Origins

Efron's journey into the realm of theatre was the first step in his ascension. When he immersed himself in the vivid world of The Great American Melodrama and Vaudeville, the doors of opportunity opened. He polished his acting skills on the intimate stage, setting the groundwork for a career that would soon captivate audiences worldwide. Efron discovered his love for performance in the sacred halls of theatrical expression, fuelled by the acclaim and connection with a live audience.

His early theatrical experiences served as a breeding environment for the raw talent that would later become synonymous with his name. Efron's journey through theatre not only shaped his craft but also ingrained in him a strong passion for the art of narrative, from captivating local audiences in Arroyo Grande to laying the stage for a Hollywood debut.

Moving on to Television

The leap from small-town theatres to the broad world of television was a watershed moment in Efron's blossoming career. In the early 2000s, he navigated the competitive terrain of television with guest appearances on shows including Firefly, ER, and The Guardian. These early roles showcased his flexibility and laid the groundwork for a bright career in front of the camera.

Efron's career took a big turn in 2004 when he secured a recurring part in the first season of the WB sitcom Summerland. This was a watershed moment for him, catapulting him from sporadic guest appearances to a more prominent position in the television world. His dedication to the art and ability to capture the soul of his characters struck a chord with both audiences and industry insiders.

Efron's proving ground was the television landscape, where he honed his acting skills and established his ability to command attention on the tiny screen. Efron's transition from theatre to television was a deliberate move that established the framework for what would become a spectacular rise in the entertainment world.

As he accepted the challenges and opportunities that television provided, Efron's personality and talent became more apparent. He honed the skills that would later make him a household name during this era. His acting abilities were shown on the tiny screen, but he also hinted at the star power that would soon define his Hollywood presence.

Chapter Two of Zac Efron's journey, in retrospect, illustrates the formative years of a young actor negotiating the convoluted routes of theatre stages and television sets. From the humble beginnings of small theatres to the far-reaching reach of television, Efron's rise in Hollywood was distinguished by hard work, early successes, and a never-ending pursuit of his dream. Little did he know that these early chapters were just the beginning of a spectacular career that would play out on both the big and small screens, enthralling audiences all over the world.

The Phenomenon of High School Musical

Few pop culture phenomena have left as permanent an imprint as the "High School Musical" series, which was anchored by Zac Efron's captivating portrayal of Troy Bolton. This chapter dives into the casting process that landed Efron the iconic part, as well as the impact it had on his career trajectory and public image.

Troy Bolton Casting: The Journey to Stardom

Zac Efron's meteoric rise can be traced back to the critical time in his career when he was cast as Troy Bolton in the Disney Channel's "High School Musical" (2006). The casting procedure was not without difficulties, as the role required a flawless blend of acting, singing, and dancing abilities. Efron's audition not only demonstrated his unquestionable talent, but also displayed a natural excitement for the idea that the casting directors appreciated.

Efron was shifting from supporting roles to potential leading man status at the moment. His casting as Troy Bolton, a high school basketball player with unexpected musical ambitions, was a lucky convergence of ability and opportunity. The chemistry he shared with co-star Vanessa Hudgens, who played Gabriella Montez, was palpable from the beginning, laying the groundwork for the film's eventual success.

Behind the Scenes: Obstacles and Victories

While Efron's vocal abilities were important in the role's musical aspects, it's worth noting that some of his singing parts in the first film were dubbed by Drew Seeley. This unique component of the production emphasises the precise efforts put in to create a cohesive musical experience. In his later musical endeavours, Efron would take on a more major vocal part, demonstrating his flexibility.

Impact on Efron's Career and Image: A Game-Changing Moment

"High School Musical" was more than just a film; it was a cultural phenomenon that went beyond its Disney Channel roots. Efron's portrayal of Troy Bolton became linked with the success of the film, propelling him into the spotlight. The film's huge appeal among adolescent audiences propelled Efron to heartthrob status almost overnight. His career was transformed, as he went from relative obscurity to A-list notoriety.

How to Navigate the Teen Idol Image

The issue of navigating a teen idol image came with sudden recognition. Efron's clean-cut, boy-next-door appeal drew him to a wide demographic, particularly young fans enamoured with the film's love escapades. However, as Efron would later reflect, this adoration was a double-edged blade. The potential of being stereotyped as a young heartthrob loomed big, threatening to limit the range of roles he might play.

Musical Development and Professional Advancement

"High School Musical"'s popularity cleared the path for sequels, with Efron repeating the role in "High School Musical 2" (2007) and "High School Musical 3: Senior Year" (2008). These films not only cemented Efron's status as a bankable star, but also displayed his maturing talents. The move of the series from television to the big screen was a watershed moment in Efron's career, showcasing his ability to carry a major motion picture.

The Success Soundtrack

Aside from the picture office success, the soundtracks to the "High School Musical" series became chart-topping hits. The combination of Efron's vocal performances and the infectious spirit of the ensemble cast contributed to the CDs' quadruple platinum certifications. This triumph emphasised Efron's crossover appeal and laid the scene for his future exploration of varied roles.

The "High School Musical" Legacy: Beyond the Teenage Dream

The legacy of "High School Musical" lives on, and its influence on Efron's career can be seen in his post-Troy Bolton selections. While some actors might have struggled to break free from the shadow of a defining part, Efron welcomed the challenge, using the franchise's success as a springboard for a diverse career.

A Versatility Platform

The unquestionable success of "High School Musical" enabled Efron to break out from the stereotype of an adolescent heartthrob. It gave him a chance to show off his flexibility as an actor, paving the way for roles that would challenge traditional assumptions. Efron's post-Troy Bolton path became a monument to his dedication to artistic growth and experimentation.

In retrospect, "High School Musical" was not just a watershed moment in Zac Efron's career, but also a watershed moment in the growth of Disney Channel Original Movies. The film's societal influence, combined with Efron's magnetic performance, continues to ring true with moviegoers, cementing its place in the pantheon of cinematic phenomena.

In the next chapters, we will look deeper into Efron's post-"High School Musical" endeavours, examining the trials and tribulations that shaped his transformation from a teenage heartthrob to a varied and renowned actor.

Hairspray and Musical Ventures

Zac Efron's foray into musical theatre constituted a watershed moment in his career, catapulting him from teen idol to multidimensional artist. This chapter dives into his musical career's progression, focusing on the transforming role he portrayed as Link Larkin in the smash film Hairspray.

Musical Career Advancement

With his debut in Disney's High School Musical franchise, Zac Efron's entry into the world of musicals was nothing short of sensational. However, it was his future undertakings that truly highlighted his musical prowess and cemented his status beyond the adolescent idol stereotype. The switch from High School Musical's legendary Troy Bolton to more diverse musical parts was a conscious decision to avoid typecasting and extend his artistic horizons.

With his performance in Hairspray (2007), Efron showed his willingness to take on hard musical roles. Based on the Broadway musical of the same name, the film cast Efron as Link Larkin, a charismatic and smooth-talking adolescent wanting to make it big on a local television dance show. This performance was a change from his basketball-centric, high school character, demonstrating his versatility as an actor.

In Hairspray, Efron not only demonstrated his singing prowess, but also his ability to immerse himself in a variety of personalities. The musical performances in the film allowed him to show off his singing and dancing abilities, indicating that he was more than simply a young heartthrob. His performance aided the film's critical and economic success, establishing him as a leading man in the musical genre.

In Hairspray, link Larkin

Zac Efron's appearance as Link Larkin in Hairspray was a watershed event for him. Link is more than simply a pretty face; he reflects the cultural and racial tensions of 1960s Baltimore. As a significant figure, Link becomes enmeshed in contemporary societal issues, notably those concerning race and integration. Efron's performance went below the surface, capturing Link's appeal as well as the dilemma he faces.

One of Efron's notable performances was his ability to depict Link's psychological difficulties through song and dance. Efron's subtle acting brought the character's progression from carefree adolescent to someone who questions conventional standards to life. The musical numbers, packed with frenetic choreography, allowed him to exhibit his dynamic range as a performer, a break from High School Musical's cloying sweetness.

Furthermore, Efron's chemistry with co-stars such as Nikki Blonsky and John Travolta enriched the ensemble cast. Link's love involvements and interactions with Tracy Turnblad, played by Blonsky, were crucial to the plot of the film. Efron's ability to communicate both young joy and societal issues of the time was critical to Hairspray's success.

The soundtrack, which featured Efron's vocals in songs like "Ladies' Choice" and "Without Love," emphasised his musical ability even more. Unlike High School Musical, where his singing portions were frequently dubbed, Hairspray used Efron's natural singing voice, proving that he could carry a musical film solely on his vocal abilities.

In retrospect, Link Larkin became a character who not only signified a difference from Efron's previous roles, but also paved the way for more diversified and mature ventures in the future. Hairspray's popularity opened opportunities in the musical genre for him, proving him as a bankable actor capable of negotiating the complexities of both character and tune.

Musical Ventures' Legacy

The section on Zac Efron's musical endeavours, particularly his appearance as Link Larkin in Hairspray, demonstrates his ability to grow as an artist. This phase was pivotal in his career, pushing him away from teen-centric parts and establishing him as a versatile actor in the entertainment world.

Efron's involvement in musicals not only emphasised his singing and dancing ability, but also his willingness to take on tough and diverse roles. The success of Hairspray laid the groundwork for subsequent ventures in which he explored the breadth of his skills, from serious roles to humorous performances. This musical chapter in Efron's career established the actor's long legacy, surpassing the constraints of early popularity.

Finally, Chapter Four peels back the layers of Zac Efron's musical journey, emphasising the importance of Hairspray in influencing his career path. The examination of Link Larkin as a character not only proved Efron's musical abilities, but also marked an important milestone in his transformation from an adolescent phenomenon to a seasoned performer ready to face the demands of the silver screen.

Musical Success After High School

Zac Efron's post-High School Musical path represented a watershed moment in his career, breaking the restrictions of his initial heartthrob image and propelling him into different parts that displayed his range as an actor. The film "17 Again," which not only emphasised Efron's comic talents but also served as a stepping stone for his progression beyond the teen idol position, was at the forefront of this transitional phase.

17 Again, released in 2009, featured Efron in a story that was different from his past efforts. This comedy-drama directed by Burr Steers starred Efron as Mike O'Donnell, a middle-aged guy magically changed back into his 17-year-old self, departing from the musical and romantic tones of High School Musical. The premise allows Efron to dig into the complexities of portraying a character caught between two ages, managing adulthood while revisiting high school.

Not only did the picture highlight Efron's comedic timing, but it also hinted at his capacity to take on more complicated parts. Mike O'Donnell's trip allowed Efron to delve into the complexities of identity and self-discovery, a departure from the simpler storylines of his earlier movies. This shift in roles was a calculated strategy, signalling to fans and industry insiders alike that Efron was ready to break free from the restrictions of his Disney-cultivated image.

One of the most remarkable features of Efron's success after High School Musical was his purposeful endeavour to broaden his filmography. The difficulties of transitioning from a young heartthrob to a more mature and nuanced actor were obvious. As he sought roles that stretched beyond the confines of his known image, Efron encountered scepticism and scrutiny. Critics and industry observers were intrigued by his ability to move beyond the established domain of musicals and embrace a broader range of genres.

Despite these obstacles, Efron displayed tenacity and a dedication to his career as an actor. The transition from Troy Bolton to characters such as Mike O'Donnell demonstrated his determination to shun stereotypes. This was a deliberate effort to reshape his career trajectory, demonstrating that he was not limited to a single genre or character archetype.

17 Again's critical and financial success reinforced Efron's strategic career choices. The film was well received by viewers, with praise for its blend of humour, heart, and Efron's captivating performance. This triumph not only cemented Efron's reputation as a bankable actor outside of the teen category, but it also opened doors to a broader range of chances in the film industry.

Role evolution did not end with 17 Again. Efron continues to pursue jobs that pushed both his acting ability and audience expectations. He experimented with genres ranging from romantic plays to thrillers, proving

his dedication to flexibility. Richard Linklater's period drama *Me and Orson Welles* (2008) and the supernatural romance drama *Charlie St. Cloud* (2010) were both notable films during this time period.
Me and Orson Welles gave Efron the opportunity to work with legendary director Richard Linklater and explore the realm of historical filmmaking. The film premiered at the Toronto International Film Festival, where it got great reviews for its historical accuracy as well as Efron's nuanced portrayal of a young man navigating the bustling world of theatre and Orson Welles' mysterious nature.

Efron welcomed the challenges of a supernatural romance drama in Charlie St. Cloud. The picture dealt with themes of love, loss, and the supernatural, which was a change from his previous roles. Efron's attention to various and hard assignments demonstrated his determination to break free from the mold of a teen star.

The difficulty of changing images extended beyond on-screen performances to public perception and industry expectations. Efron had to persuade both spectators and casting directors that he was more than just a charismatic high school basketball star. The trip necessitated a delicate balance of positions that highlighted his range while also deliberately controlling the narrative surrounding his career progression.

During this time, Efron's foray into producing through his company, Ninjas Runnin' Wild, was also crucial. The engagement of the company in the production of films such as *Dirty Grandpa* (2016), *That Awkward Moment* (2014), and *Extremely Wicked, Shockingly Evil and Vile* (2019) underlined Efron's devotion to crafting his own career path. These projects allowed him to experiment with different aspects of filmmaking and contribute to narratives that reflected his changing artistic sensibility.

However, the issues of changing image were not without their share of complaints and controversy. Some questioned whether Efron could successfully discard his Disney persona, while others questioned the long-term viability of his switch to more mature roles. The media and public scrutiny grew, amplifying Efron's every move as he navigated this important stage of his career.

Finally, Chapter Five of Zac Efron's biography reveals a watershed moment in his career defined by the success of *17 Again* and a purposeful shift in roles. The chapter digs not just into the artistic complexities of his performances, but also into the strategic considerations and obstacles associated with rebuilding his image in Hollywood's merciless terrain. Efron's post-High School Musical trajectory demonstrates his tenacity, artistic maturation, and drive to leave a lasting legacy beyond the dazzle of juvenile success.

Broadening The Horizons

In the progression of Zac Efron's career, Chapter Six is a significant study of the actor's conscious shift into tragic parts, most notably in "Me and Orson Welles" and "Charlie St. Cloud." This chapter delves into the complexities of Efron's path as he moves away from the teen heartthrob image formed by the success of High School Musical and into unknown territory in the field of cinematic narrative.

Orson Welles and Me: A Theatrical Odyssey

One of the turning points in Efron's career was the 2008 film "Me and Orson Welles." The picture, directed by Richard Linklater, thrust Efron into the domain of period drama, a departure from the modern settings he had become accustomed to. The story is set in the theatrical milieu of 1937 New York and revolves around a young aspiring actor, played by Efron, who secures a role in Orson Welles' innovative production of Shakespeare's "Julius Caesar."

Efron's portrayal of the ambitious and idealistic Richard Samuels is a nuanced performance that hints at the actor's range outside of the musical and comedy areas. The film not only allowed Efron to work alongside established performers like as Christian McKay and Claire Danes, but it also allowed him to immerse himself in the complexities of historical narrative. "Me and Orson Welles" received excellent reviews for Efron's performance and revealed his potential for a wider range of roles.

Charlie St. Cloud: A Supernatural Journey

Following the success of "Me and Orson Welles," Efron pushed himself even further with the 2010 picture "Charlie St. Cloud." Burr Steers directed this drama, which deviated from traditional storylines by incorporating mystical elements into the plot. Efron played Charlie, a young guy dealing with grief following the death of his younger brother. What distinguishes this picture is Charlie's capacity to connect with his departed sibling, an idea that adds a mystical and emotional element to the story.

"Charlie St. Cloud" demonstrates Efron's ability to communicate a wide range of emotions, delving into the depths of grief and the complications of moving on after a big loss. The picture explores themes of love, redemption, and the supernatural, giving Efron a chance to show off his theatrical abilities. While not without controversy, Efron's performance in "Charlie St. Cloud" proved him as an actor capable of handling roles requiring a delicate balance of emotional depth and fanciful storytelling.

Exploring Dramatic Roles: A Cinematic Evolution

The shift from musicals and comedies to period dramas and ghostly stories was an intentional effort on Efron's side to break free from the restrictions of his previous image. These films demonstrated his dedication to perfecting his craft as an actor capable of producing engaging performances across a wide range of genres. Efron's purposeful decision to take on jobs that veered from the typical trajectory of a former Disney star revealed his commitment to artistic growth and a desire to be recognised for his acting abilities rather than his heartthrob reputation.

These forays into the dramatic area not only widened Efron's skill set, but also allowed him to work with seasoned directors and actors, fostering a learning atmosphere that would be crucial for his future efforts. The critical response to these films indicated a progressive acceptance of Efron in more serious and layered characters, encouraging filmmakers to consider him for projects outside the scope of his previous hits.

Chapter Six, which chronicles Efron's entry into dramatic parts, exemplifies the actor's resolve to surpass the confines of his first fame. "Me and Orson Welles" and "Charlie St. Cloud" became landmarks in his career, displaying a depth and emotional resonance that pointed at a promising future in serious cinema. These films provided the groundwork for Efron's later phases of his career, in which he proceeded to explore numerous genres, finally cementing his image as a multidimensional actor capable of enthralling viewers across a range of storytelling approaches. The chapter not only illustrates Efron's artistic progress, but it also sets the stage for the trials and victories that lie ahead for him in the following chapters.

Production Company and Digital Content Production

Ninjas Runnin' Wild: Efron's Production Company and Digital Content Production Chapter Seven: The Entrepreneurial Side

Zac Efron's career in the entertainment industry extends beyond his on-screen roles. Chapter Seven dives into the actor's entrepreneurial side, examining the formation and operation of his production firm, Ninjas Runnin' Wild, as well as his entry into the world of digital content production.

Ninjas Gone Wild: The Inception of a Production Powerhouse

In 2010, Efron started his own production company, Ninjas Runnin' Wild, which he named after himself. This decision demonstrated Efron's willingness to be a performer as well as have a creative say in the projects he brings to life. With the formation of a production firm, he was able to directly participate in the development and execution of film projects, constructing narratives that spoke to both himself and audiences.

The title "Ninjas Runnin' Wild" suggests a sense of excitement and unpredictability, as well as a willingness to take chances and explore different storytelling approaches. This decision illustrates Efron's dedication to pushing boundaries and connecting with content that defies traditional assumptions.

Efron's Project Development Participation

One of the most important parts of Ninjas Runnin' Wild is Efron's involvement in project development. The chapter discusses how Efron uses his industry knowledge and creative intuition to select promising screenplays and themes. He has the ability to interact with developing and established talents through the production firm, contributing to a varied range of projects that correspond with his artistic vision.

This section delves into particular instances where Efron's influence affected the trajectory of Ninjas Runnin' Wild flicks. Efron's job as a producer takes front stage in this chapter, from selecting scripts that correspond with his developing career aspirations to supporting movies that resonate with bigger societal concerns.

Expanding the Horizons of Digital Content Production

Traditional boundaries in the entertainment scene have blurred in the digital age, allowing content makers to experiment with new formats. Chapter Seven focuses on Efron's entry into digital content production.

The chapter describes how Ninjas Runnin' Wild reacted to a shifting industry landscape by diversifying into digital content. This covers not only traditional film production but also the creation of online content for a worldwide audience. Efron's strategic alliance with digital platforms indicates a knowledge of the changing dynamics of content consumption as well as the importance of reaching viewers outside of traditional cinema.

Channels on YouTube: "Off the Grid" and "Gym Time"

In March 2019, Efron expanded his digital presence by starting his own YouTube channel. The chapter delves at the origins of this channel and its significance to Efron's entire brand. Two weekly episodes, "Off the Grid" and "Gym Time," provide viewers with insight into various aspects of Efron's life.

"Off the Grid" takes viewers on outdoor activities, demonstrating Efron's commitment to living life outside of the confines of contemporary technology. This series not only corresponds with current trends that emphasise outdoor adventures, but it also displays Efron as a relatable character negotiating the intricacies of a tech-dominated world.

"Gym Time," on the other hand, gives a behind-the-scenes peek at Efron's exercise and dietary regimes. This series not only caters to fitness fans, but it also underlines Efron's commitment to living a healthy lifestyle. The chapter goes into how these programmes have been received, examining how they contribute to Efron's brand and resonate with a varied audience.

Platform Dynamics and Backlash

The introduction of Efron's YouTube channel, however, was not without controversy. The chapter delves into the response from some members of the YouTube community who accuse the platform of favouring famous celebrities over lesser-known producers. This occurrence calls into question the dynamics of celebrity impact in the digital sphere, as well as the difficulties that established individuals confront when stepping into channels normally dominated by emerging creators.

Ninjas on the Run in the Digital Age

In the chapter's last sections, the emphasis changes to Ninjas Runnin' Wild's larger strategy in the digital age. How does Efron's production firm tackle the hurdles of online content development while also remaining active in traditional filmmaking? The chapter delves into Efron's strategic decisions, alliances, and the overall impact of Ninjas Runnin' Wild on his career as an actor and content producer.

Chapter Seven focuses on Zac Efron's entrepreneurial endeavours, depicting him as a versatile thinker influencing narratives both on and off the screen. From the inception of Ninjas Runnin' Wild to the exploration of digital content realms, Efron's production path demonstrates his dedication to artistic expression and innovation in an ever-changing industry. This chapter encourages readers to see the intersection of creativity, entrepreneurship, and digital discovery in Zac Efron's intriguing world.

Trials and Triumphs

Even the brightest stars cast shadows on their personal lives in the sparkling world of Hollywood, where the spotlight never dims. Despite his dazzling on-screen personality and accomplishment, Zac Efron has faced tremendous personal challenges while under the constant light of public scrutiny. This chapter dives into the ups and downs that have shaped Efron's life, highlighting the perseverance and fortitude that lay beyond the famous façade.

Personal Struggles: An Insider's Account

Zac Efron's rise to fame was not without difficulties. He became an overnight hit as the heartthrob of the High School Musical franchise, grabbing the hearts of youngsters all over the world. However, the quick climb to stardom came with it a set of pressures and expectations that extended beyond the screen. In an honest admission, Efron admitted to struggling with the constant quest of perfection during his early career. The ambition for academic brilliance, combined with the continual examination of his public image, generated an internal conflict that drove him to "flip out" at the slightest mention of a grade lower than a "A."

This internal turmoil reached a climax when Efron found himself at a crossroads of personal and professional pressures while striving to balance academic goals and a blossoming acting career. The urge to conform to cultural expectations collided with the reality of a young actor navigating the turbulent waters of celebrity. This moment of internal strife would pave the way for more fundamental challenges in Efron's life.

In the midst of glittering premieres and rapturous hoopla, Efron battled alcoholism and substance abuse. In 2013, he bravely sought treatment, marking a watershed moment in his life. The revelation of his troubles served as a reminder that superstars, like everyone else, deal with the same human vulnerabilities. When Efron experienced a big setback in November 2013, a fall at home resulted in a broken jaw, resulting in his mouth being wired shut, the story took an unexpected turn. This near-fatal tragedy highlighted the depth of his personal issues and the toll that fame can exact.

Public Scrutiny: Celebrity's Double-Edged Sword

A celebrity's life, especially one who rose to popularity at an early age, is a double-edged sword. The currency of celebrity is public love, but it comes with an unavoidable flip side: the scrutiny of every act, choice, and failure. In the middle of his personal struggles, Efron found himself under the constant scrutiny of the media and the public. The tabloid media dissected his struggles, sensationalising the very real difficulties he encountered.

The 2014 incident on Skid Row, in which Efron got into a violent struggle with a homeless guy, made headlines. Law enforcement refrained from making arrests, regarding it as mutual warfare, but the incident fed the media's unquenchable hunger for celebrity scandal. Efron's vulnerability became fodder for gossip columns, and the story of a young celebrity dealing with personal demons eclipsed the story of perseverance and recovery.

As Efron freely disclosed his experiences with transcendental meditation (TM) as a coping strategy, the criticism increased. While the practice provided him with a haven in the midst of upheaval, it also became a source of suspicion and criticism. The unwavering public gaze alternated between empathy and judgement, displaying the complex dance celebrities do on the tightrope of personal discovery.

Overcoming Adversity: A Resilience Journey

Zac Efron's path through personal adversity exemplifies the human capacity for resilience. Despite being heightened by fame, the struggles parallel the human experience of overcoming hardship. Efron's devotion to sobriety since June 2013 marks a watershed moment in his life. It's a story about overcoming personal demons, with the teenage idol of High School Musical transformed into a symbol of resilience.

Efron's candour in sharing his struggles attracted him to followers and humanised the superstar persona. His choice to go public about his mental health difficulties in 2022, exposing battles with insomnia, agoraphobia, and depression, shattered the illusion of invincibility even further. As a result, he became a champion for mental health awareness, using his position to de-stigmatize conversations about mental health.

Beyond the turbulent years, Efron's transfer to Australia in 2021 represented a watershed moment in his life. Stepping away from the Hollywood rush, he took refuge in the serenity of Byron Bay, reflecting a deliberate attempt to prioritise mental and emotional well-being over the trappings of famous life. This geographical movement emphasises Efron's commitment to personal development and a purposeful step away from the spotlight, which previously both lit and scrutinised his every action.

Zac Efron's tribulations and accomplishments serve as a heartbreaking account of the human experience within the celebrity labyrinth in a world where storylines frequently bounce between admiration and scandal. Efron's journey transcends the screen, resonating with the collective problems of individuals navigating the complexity of life in the public eye, from the dizzying heights of teenage heartthrob to the depths of personal struggles.

This chapter reveals a guy who, despite the dazzling lights of Hollywood, fought his own shadows and emerged not as a faultless idol but as a strong human being. Through personal adversity, Zac Efron rewrites the triumphant story, demonstrating that even in the most publicised conflicts, winning rests in vulnerability, resilience, and the willingness to reveal one's real experience.

Beyond the Movies

Zac Efron has not only graced the silver screen with his charming presence, but has also moved into new territory, exhibiting versatility that transcends beyond the world of traditional acting. This chapter dives into two important aspects of Efron's career during this period: his study of the streaming world via Netflix's "Down to Earth with Zac Efron" and his entry into voice acting.

Down to Earth with Zac Efron on Netflix

In 2020, Efron embarked on a world tour with the Netflix documentary series "Down to Earth with Zac Efron." Efron embraced the role of a travel aficionado and environmental champion, displaying a side of himself rarely seen by the public, departing from his typical parts in scripted movies.

The eight-episode series follows Efron and wellness expert Darin Olien as they travel the world in search of sustainable and eco-friendly methods. From Iceland to Costa Rica, the team immerses themselves in various cultures, spotlighting local projects promoting environmental conservation, sustainable energy, and holistic well-being.

What distinguishes "Down to Earth" is Efron's genuine curiosity and eagerness to learn. Viewers witness a change from Hollywood's glitz and glamour, showcasing Efron's down-to-earth demeanour and his commitment for making a positive influence on the globe. The show not only entertains but also educates viewers, pushing them to choose sustainable lifestyle options.

Efron's transformation from heartthrob actor to eco-conscious traveller may appear surprising, but it is consistent with an increasing trend in the entertainment industry in which celebrities use their celebrity to promote social and environmental causes. "Down to Earth" not only adds a new dimension to Efron's career, but also places him as a prominent voice for environmental awareness.

Exploring Voice Acting

Aside from his on-screen presence, Efron has also taken on the challenge of voice acting, providing his vocal talents to animated characters. While some performers may see it as a step away from the spotlight, Efron appreciated the chance to express emotion and personality only through his voice.

Efron voiced Fred Jones in Warner Bros.' animated film "Scoob!" in 2020, a modern twist on the iconic Scooby-Doo franchise. To play an iconic character like Fred, Efron had to change his style, relying on intonation, expressiveness, and timing to bring the character to life without the use of physical motions or facial expressions.

Voice acting presents performers with a unique set of challenges and opportunities, asking them to harness their creativity in a new way. Efron's foray into this world not only demonstrates his versatility, but also broadens his repertory, demonstrating that his abilities transcend beyond the visual components of performance.

The decision to do voice acting demonstrates Efron's readiness to take on diverse projects that will test his abilities and widen his artistic horizons. It demonstrates his commitment to industry expansion, proving that he is not willing to rest on the laurels of his previous triumphs.

Efron's study of these options positions him as a dynamic and forward-thinking artist as the entertainment environment continues to expand with the rise of streaming platforms and animated features. Whether he's narrating an animated character's travels or immersing himself in global exploration on a documentary series, Efron's desire to push the boundaries of his profession signals a new chapter in his career.

In Chapter Nine, we see Zac Efron abandon Hollywood's scripted narratives in favour of unscripted storytelling and animated realms. "Down to Earth with Zac Efron" not only demonstrates his love for sustainable living, but it also solidifies his image as a celebrity with a mission. Simultaneously, his foray into voice acting demonstrates his adaptability and dedication to studying the diverse nature of the entertainment industry.

This chapter exemplifies Efron's progress as an artist who navigates the industry's shifting currents while remaining true to his core ideals. As we go beyond the silver screen, we discover Zac Efron not only entertaining but also inspiring viewers with his dedication to meaningful storytelling and willingness to accept the many chances that come his way.

A Journey Through Australia

A significant chapter in Zac Efron's life unfolds as he goes on an Australian expedition, signalling a revolutionary phase in his personal and professional career. The decision to relocate to Australia reflects a mix of curiosity, adventure, and a need for reinvention, as it trades the familiar Hollywood scene for the immensity of the Australian continent.

Moving to Australia: A Daring Step into the Unknown

The idea of Hollywood stars seeking refuge and new starts in far-flung locations is not new, but Efron's decision to make Australia his home has a special resonance. The announcement, made in early 2021, prompted a surge of conjecture and intrigue. Efron sought peace away from the glitz of Los Angeles in the tranquil coastal hamlet of Byron Bay. The causes for this geographical shift were as varied as his new surroundings' landscapes.

Australia, with its laid-back lifestyle and untouched natural beauty, presented Efron with a respite from Hollywood's frenzied pace. The choice to immerse himself in the Australian way of life was more than just a change of scenery; it was a conscious step towards a more grounded lifestyle. Efron discovered a sense of obscurity away from the continual spotlight, a valuable commodity for someone who had spent the most of his life in the public view.

The actor's ties to Australia were strengthened when he purchased a home in Byron Bay, a coastal enclave noted for its gorgeous beaches and lush hinterland. The relocation to Australia represented not only a change of residence, but also a significant shift in attitude, a deliberate effort to restore equilibrium in a world dominated by extremes.

Australian Projects: Embracing a New Creative Landscape

As Efron settled into his new home in Australia, the question lingered: What would this move entail for his career? The answer came in the form of a succession of films that demonstrated Efron's versatility and readiness to embrace the different options of the Australian entertainment industry.

Gold (2022), directed by Anthony Hayes, was Efron's first journey into the harsh Australian outback. Efron had to delve into the nuances of survival and human nature for the picture, which was set against the backdrop of a gold mine. The selection of such a grim and intense project indicated Efron's ambition to push himself, adopting tales that went beyond the expected.

Concurrently, Efron starred in Firestarter, a remake of the 1984 blockbuster based on Stephen King's novel. This production, directed by Keith Thomas, allowed Efron to explore the darker corners of cinema, bringing his star power to a genre that frequently requires a visceral connection with the viewer. The Australian setting adds a distinct flavour to the story, reworking a classic story amid the haunted landscapes of Australia.

The Greatest Beer Run Ever, a Vietnam War-set comedy directed by Peter Farrelly, broadened Efron's Australian ventures even more. This project demonstrated Efron's ability to move fluidly between genres, from horror to historical comedy, demonstrating his dedication to a broad profession.

Aside from these cinematic endeavours, Efron continued to explore the various opportunities available in the Australian entertainment industry. His participation in the future film The Iron Claw, directed by Sean Durkin, cemented his place in Australian cinema. The picture, centred on the Von Erich wrestling family, promised to dive into a unique aspect of storytelling, fitting with Efron's affinity for narratives that push boundaries.

Beyond the screen, Efron's move was distinguished by involvement with the local community. His presence in Australia extended beyond film sets, with tales of him attending community events and embracing the laid-back Aussie way of life. This immersion in his new surroundings showed more than simply a professional devotion, but also a true incorporation into the fabric of Australian life.

The Impact and Reception of Cultural Fusion

Efron's trip to Australia sparked debate not only about his career choices, but also about the changing dynamics of the global entertainment industry. The move represented a shift from conventional centres of fame, calling into question the concept that success in Hollywood was associated with success internationally.

The influence of Efron's Australian chapter was felt not just by fans, but also by industry insiders who recognised the importance of worldwide cooperation. Working on Australian projects showed a desire to contribute to cross-cultural storytelling, adding a layer of cultural richness to his body of work.

Furthermore, Efron's appearance elicited both curiosity and warmth in Australia. The actor's ability to blend into the Australian creative landscape without overshadowing local talent demonstrated a collaborative attitude. His participation in projects that highlighted Australian tales while appealing to a worldwide audience demonstrated a nuanced approach to cultural fusion.

As Chapter Ten of Zac Efron's life comes to a close, the actor's Australian journey exemplifies his tenacity, adaptability, and constant commitment to artistic inquiry. The move to Australia was more than just a change of residence; it was a calculated step towards self-discovery and creative renewal.

Efron's desire to venture into the unknown, both geographically and creatively, reflects a larger theme in his life—a never-ending search for progress and authenticity. With its numerous initiatives and cultural immersion, the Australian chapter adds a rich depth to the story of a man who refuses to be constrained by the expectations of stardom.

As the actor continues to explore uncharted territory in his profession, one thing becomes clear: Zac Efron's Australian voyage is a continuation of a journey distinguished by change, discovery, and an undying passion for the craft. The story, far from ending, unfolds with the promise of new vistas and the limitless possibilities of an unrestrained creative soul.

Battles and Transformations in Health

Zac Efron's path in the spotlight has been distinguished not only by the glitz and glamour of Hollywood, but also by profound health challenges and transformative situations that have impacted the actor beyond his on-screen appearances. This chapter dives into his hardships, from substance misuse to his amazing recovery, as well as the deep intersections of his physical and mental health journeys.

Substance Abuse and Rehabilitation

The temptation of celebrity frequently has its drawbacks, and Efron found himself navigating the perilous waters of substance abuse. The actor suffered the difficulties that come with stardom under the harsh scrutiny of the public light. The leap from teen heartthrob to more mature parts in High School Musical brought with it the hurdles of reinvention and cultural expectations.

Efron's candour regarding his struggles with alcoholism and substance misuse was a watershed moment in his career. The chapter delves into the events that lead to his troubles, the impact on his personal and professional life, and his brave determination to tackle his demons head on. The story unfolds with true honesty, describing the moments of vulnerability that preceded his recovery process.

The actor's decision to get treatment in early 2013 showed a dedication to personal development and well-being. Interviews and public statements provide readers with insight into the rehabilitation process, allowing them to see the strength required to break free from the grasp of addiction. The chapter dives into the support systems that were critical to Efron's recovery, emphasising the value of friends, family, and professional advice.

Physical and Mental Health Adventures

Beyond his difficulties with substance misuse, Zac Efron's health story takes a complex turn, combining physical and mental well-being. Efron had a major setback in November 2013 when he had to have his jaw wired shut due to a tumble at home. This occurrence, which was first shrouded in mystery, is investigated in depth, revealing the facts surrounding the fall and the ensuing repercussions on Efron's life.

The fact that Efron nearly died during the event in 2022 adds a sad depth to his journey. Readers are invited to see the actor's tenacity as he deals with the fall's aftermath, musing on the frailty of life and the unexpected turns that might define one's fate. The story delves into the incident's emotional and physical toll, presenting a nuanced view of Efron's public persona against the internal hardships he suffered.

While filming his adventure series "Killing Zac Efron" in Papua New Guinea in December 2019, the actor contracted a dangerous and potentially fatal sickness characterised as a "form of typhoid or similar bacterial infection." This section of the chapter delves into the difficulties he faced while dealing with illness in a strange nation, the medical interventions that followed, and the influence on both his physical health and the series' production.

Efron's candour regarding his mental health issues adds another element to the story. The actor opened up about his struggles with insomnia, agoraphobia, and depression, emphasising the toll his job had on his health. The constant pursuit of physical transformations for jobs, such as taking diuretics for Baywatch, contributed to the development of severe mental health issues. The chapter delves into the delicate balance of the entertainment industry's demands and the toll it can take on an individual's mental health.

"Health Battles and Transformations" offers a complete picture of Zac Efron's tenacity in the face of hardship. The actor's journey becomes a monument to the complexity of celebrity, the impact of societal expectations, and the significance of prioritising one's well-being through the highs and lows. The chapter finishes by focusing on Efron's growth as a person who found strength in vulnerability, motivating others to face their own problems with courage and honesty. Zac Efron emerges not only as an actor but also as a survivor in this investigation of health challenges and transformations, reminding us all that true transformation often necessitates braving the darkest depths of one's own life.

A Star with Many Faces

Zac Efron is a beacon of flexibility and talent in the glittering world of Hollywood, where stars rise and fall like constellations in the night sky. This chapter dives into his various prizes and achievements, as well as the enormous influence he has had on popular culture.

Awards & Recognition

Zac Efron's rise from a teenage actor with a penchant for musicals to a versatile star has been marked by industry recognition and admiration. His awards demonstrate not just his acting ability, but also his ability to play a variety of characters.

The phenomenal success of the High School Musical franchise was a watershed moment in Efron's career. Although the critical reaction was divided at first, the impact on adolescent audiences was apparent. The movie won numerous honours, including a Teen Choice Award for Choice TV Breakout Star for Efron's depiction of Troy Bolton, the confused high school heartthrob. This marked the start of Efron's ascension into the hearts of fans and industry insiders alike.

His roles expanded as his career progressed. Efron's flexibility was highlighted by his crossover from the teen song genre to more mature and demanding ventures. In 2017, he was nominated for a Golden Globe Award for Best Actor in a Musical or Comedy for his portrayal in The Greatest

Showman, a musical drama based on the life of P.T. Barnum. This nomination not only recognised Efron's progress as an actor, but also established him as a contender for more challenging roles.

Efron's desire to venture into uncharted territory did not go unnoticed. He received critical acclaim for his portrayal of serial killer Ted Bundy in Extremely Wicked, Shockingly Evil, and Vile. Despite mixed reviews, Efron's performance was praised for its intricacy and divergence from his past performances. This remarkable performance earned him awards and cemented his reputation as an actor who isn't afraid to push the boundaries of his own profession.

Efron's influence extends beyond the usual awards circuit, as seen by his contributions to the film business. In 2021, he won a Daytime Emmy Award for Outstanding Daytime Programme Host for his involvement in Down to Earth with Zac Efron, a Netflix travel show. This surprising breakthrough in hosting demonstrated Efron's ability to interact with people on a different platform, demonstrating that his magnetism extends beyond written acts.

Efron's Influence on Pop Culture

Zac Efron's meteoric rise transcends the screen, leaving an enduring imprint on popular culture. Efron became a cultural sensation, particularly among the millennial population, thanks to his signature Troy Bolton hair flip and the infectious lyrics of High School Musical.

High School Musical, in particular, has become a cultural icon. The captivating tunes, relatable teen drama, and Efron's charming presence propelled him into the hearts of teenage fans all around the world. The impact extended beyond the movies, influencing fashion trends, igniting dance crazes, and cementing Efron's status as a teen idol.

However, Efron's impact on pop culture extends far beyond his days as a teen darling. His progression into more mature roles reflected the maturation of his audience. The change involved not just abandoning his "Disney pretty boy" persona, but also navigating the realities of maturity. This voyage struck a chord with followers who had grown up watching him on film, forging a link that transcended the fleeting nature of stardom.

Efron's involvement in content creation through his production firm, Ninjas Runnin' Wild, demonstrates his dedication to altering the cultural landscape. Efron embraced new channels in an era dominated by digital media, producing content that represents his interests and engages a varied audience. Fans were able to engage with Efron on a more personal level thanks to the creation of his YouTube channel, which featured series such as "Off the Grid" and "Gym Time," blurring the barriers between celebrity and spectator.

His migration to Australia and the projects he worked on there became part of his story, influencing talks not only about his career but also about the attractiveness of a different way of life. The media coverage of Efron's Australian adventure contributed to the continuing debate about celebrities choosing a quieter life away from the Hollywood glare, adding to the changing dynamics of fame and public image.

In terms of health and lifestyle, Efron's candour regarding his battles with drinking, substance addiction, and mental health endeared him to followers who were going through similar issues. His support for well-being and open comments about personal struggles revealed a sensitivity rarely seen in the glitzy world of stardom. This candour struck a chord with audiences, creating a bond that extends beyond the roles he performs on screen.

In conclusion, Zac Efron's rise from High School Musical breakout star to multidimensional actor, producer, and cultural influencer demonstrates his versatility and enduring appeal. The honours and accolades he has received over the course of his career are more than just tokens of industry acknowledgment; they are also landmarks in a trajectory that continues to shape and be shaped by popular culture. Efron's influence extends beyond the characters he plays; it is based on his ability to adapt, connect, and leave an indelible impression on the ever-changing canvas of entertainment and culture.

Jewish Heritage

Zac Efron, the charming actor known for his roles in High School Musical, The Greatest Showman, and a slew of other films, brings a rich area of background with him that reaches beyond Hollywood's gloss and glamour. His Jewish history, which frequently takes a back seat to his on-screen endeavours, lends dimension to his character. Exploring Efron's past reveals a tale of cultural roots, familial bonds, and the subtle discovery of identity.

The surname "Efron" is a linguistic lighthouse, vibrating with Hebrew cadence. The name's derivation takes us to the heart of Jewish culture, offering a glimpse into a centuries-old tradition. This language ties Efron to a tradition that predates the silver screen and the entertainment industry. It's a link that screams of common history and struggles.

What makes this story interesting is the junction of ancestry and personal belief. Despite his Jewish surname, Efron's relationship with Judaism is complicated. Efron's relationship to Judaism surpasses the rituals and customs generally connected with the faith. He was raised in an agnostic atmosphere where religious practices were not a big aspect of his youth.

In identifying as Jewish, Efron expresses a cultural identification that transcends beyond religious affiliation. It becomes a lens through which he sees himself, an acknowledgment of a lineage that moulds his viewpoint. The acceptance of Jewish identity demonstrates the multifaceted character of legacy – a fusion of cultural, historical, and familial factors that mix into a distinct individual identity.

Given his upbringing outside of religious practice, one would wonder about the relevance of Efron's affinity with Judaism. This affiliation becomes an exploration, a deliberate decision to embrace a part of his lineage that crosses religious bounds. It emphasises the flexibility of identity and the freedom that individuals have in crafting their own story.

The investigation into Efron's Jewish heritage also raises questions about the importance of cultural identity in a world that frequently divides people based on their beliefs. In a culture where labels may be oppressive, Efron's embrace of his Jewish background becomes a statement — an assertion of identity that transcends preconceived assumptions.

Furthermore, this investigation sparks a broader conversation regarding the diversity of religious and cultural identities. Despite not actively practicing the religion, Efron's Jewish identity challenges preconceptions and offers a more nuanced understanding of what it means to belong to a particular cultural or religious community. It represents the idea that identity is a dynamic interplay of human decision, family history, and cultural resonance rather than a rigid construct.

The interaction between heritage and personal belief is a delicate ballet that Efron's story enables us to observe. It elicits thoughts about how people negotiate the tapestry of their identities, plucking threads from various strands to weave their own story. In this story, Efron's Jewish heritage becomes a vibrant thread in the greater mosaic of his identity.

The actor's journey serves as a reminder that legacy is a spectrum of influences that shape an individual, rather than a single entity. Efron's link to Judaism becomes a celebration of cultural identity diversity, emphasising that there is no single way to embody or express one's background. It's a story that promotes a more inclusive sense of identity that is free of rigid categorizations.

Finally, the investigation into Zac Efron's Jewish ancestry reveals a story that goes beyond the surface of a surname. It's a story about belonging - to language, culture, and a historical legacy that transcends time. Despite his non-religious background, Efron's self-identification as Jewish defies society standards and pushes us to reconsider the flexibility of identity. In this investigation, we discover not just a Hollywood celebrity, but a person whose life embodies the complicated dance between heritage and personal choice, a ballet that has ramifications far beyond the bounds of the silver screen.

Academic Excellence

Zac Efron's rise to fame and acclaim has been distinguished not only by his charismatic appearance on screen, but also by his dedication to academic success. Beyond Hollywood's flash and glamour, Efron's early years indicate a resolve to excel not only as an entertainer but also as a committed student.

Academic prowess was visible in the corridors of Arroyo Grande High School, where Efron spent his formative years. The contrast between his life as a student and his growing interest in acting set the stage for a remarkable balancing act that would influence his career.

Efron was raised in a middle-class home and enjoyed what he characterised as a "normal childhood." His father, an electrical engineer, and mother, an administrative assistant, created a solid foundation for Efron when he was young. This background, combined with a sibling dynamic that included a younger brother, Dylan, and a half-sister, Olivia, created a supportive environment for study.

Efron's dedication to academic success is demonstrated by his own admission that he would "flip out" if he received a "B" grade instead of a "A." This mindset, which he developed during his school years, demonstrated a level of dedication and drive that would eventually define not only his academic endeavours, but also his approach to the problems of the entertainment industry.

Efron's usual high school career took an unexpected turn when he became captivated by the world of theatre. The Great American Melodrama and Vaudeville became his stage, and Efron began developing his acting skills under the tutelage of his drama teacher, Robyn Metchik. Metchik's endorsement led him to an agent in Los Angeles, marking his first steps into the world of professional acting.

Efron continued to manage the scholastic rigours of high school while his enthusiasm for the theatre and screen intensified. His 2006 graduation from Arroyo Grande High School demonstrated his ability to properly balance the demands of both environments. This feat also provided Efron with the opportunity to attend the University of Southern California.

Despite the possibility of furthering his formal education, Efron chose a different path. He declined enrollment at USC due to the draw of Hollywood and the rising potential in the entertainment industry. Instead, he chose to plunge completely into the world of acting, a decision that would quickly propel him into the spotlight.

Even as his acting career took off, Efron's dedication to academic success remained unwavering. Being a Hollywood heartthrob and an intellectually oriented individual is an aspect of his personality that distinguishes him. It debunks the idea of celebrities who are entirely focused on their craft, demonstrating that intelligence and artistic ability may coexist.

Early parts in television programmes such as "Firefly," "ER," and "The Guardian" served as stepping stones, but it was his breakout role in "High School Musical" that catapulted him to stardom. The success of the film and its subsequent sequels established Efron as a teen idol, but despite the attention, he remained dedicated to his intellectual endeavours.

When Efron decided not to attend USC, his academic life followed a different path. Instead, he attended the Pacific Conservatory of the Performing Arts, where he honed his theatre skills. This action showed a calculated decision to combine practical knowledge with his growing celebrity, demonstrating a nuanced grasp of career progression.

As Efron negotiated the world of show business, his appearances in films such as "Hairspray" and "17 Again" were economic successes. Despite the grandeur of Hollywood premieres and red carpets, vestiges of a student who once pushed for academic excellence remained.

The contradiction of Efron's life, defined by the alternating demands of scripts and textbooks, demonstrates his ability to embrace several sides of his identity. While playing characters on television, he remained committed to continued learning.

Efron's entry into production, with the formation of his own firm, Ninjas Runnin' Wild, highlights his diverse approach to the entertainment industry. The company's involvement in the development of films such as "Dirty Grandpa" and "Extremely Wicked, Shockingly Evil and Vile" demonstrates not just his acting talent but also his strategic position as a producer.

Efron won a Daytime Emmy Award for anchoring the Netflix travel show "Down to Earth with Zac Efron" in 2021. This honour, based on his capacity to connect audiences in ways other than scripted performances, provides another layer to the story of a man who, outside the gleam of Hollywood, continues to pursue different interests.

The story of Zac Efron's academic achievement is more than just a chapter in his history; it is a story that defies preconceived beliefs about the junction of stardom and scholarly endeavours. It emphasises the idea that behind the attractive smile and enthralling performances is a person who regards education as a cornerstone of personal development.

As Efron's career progresses from HighSchool Musical heartthrob to versatile actor exploring genres, his dedication to academic success is a constant thread connecting the various chapters of his life. It serves as a reminder that, for him, the search for knowledge is an ongoing part of his story, building a legacy that stretches beyond the silver screen.

Theatre Roots

Before becoming a household name through his Hollywood triumphs, Zac Efron honed his craft in the world of theatre. His path to the performing arts was defined by a number of significant encounters that impacted not just his acting abilities but also his grasp of the entertainment industry. This investigation delves into Efron's early career, when the spotlight was a stage and the applause came from live crowds.

The Great American Melodrama and Vaudeville: The Performance Crucible

Efron was engaged in the vivid world of The Great American Melodrama and Vaudeville long before High School Musical launched him to international celebrity. This theatre in Oceano, California, became a testing ground for his budding talent. Working in such a setting gave him a one-of-a-kind apprenticeship, helping him to grasp the nuances of live performance and the immediate connection created with the audience.

Efron was not only an ambitious actor at The Great American Melodrama and Vaudeville; he became a part of a tradition that revered melodrama, a theatrical form characterised by exaggerated characters, strong moral issues, and a heightened feeling of passion. This event paved the way for his later ability to represent characters with depth and realism, even in Hollywood's frequently surreal domain.

A Symphony of Roles: Early Efron's Repertoire

The switch from melodrama to musicals was a watershed moment in Efron's career. Beyond melodrama, he demonstrated his flexibility in a number of productions. Gipsy, a classic musical that examines the world of burlesque, gave Efron a chance to stretch his acting muscles in a new direction. It demonstrated his versatility and hinted at the range he would eventually display in his Hollywood career.

Following Gipsy, Efron's theatrical credits included Peter Pan, Little Shop of Horrors, and The Music Man. These varied parts necessitated not just acting ability, but also musical ability - a facet of Efron's skill set that would become a defining characteristic in his later movie endeavours. Little did he know that these early experiences would pave the way for his breakout part in High School Musical, when his singing and acting abilities fused effortlessly.

Recommendations and Representation in the Limelight

Efron's passion and talent were observed while polishing his skills on the theatre stage. Robyn Metchik, his theatre teacher, saw his promise and referred him to a Los Angeles agent. This watershed moment signified Efron's departure from local theatre and onto the larger landscape of the entertainment industry. With the support of his newfound representation, he was ready to take on more substantial tasks in the acting profession.

The transition from regional theatre to Hollywood is difficult, but Efron's dedication to his profession and early stage experiences provided a solid foundation. After signing with the Creative Artists Agency, he began a road that would lead to auditions, callbacks, and, eventually, a breakthrough that would change his career forever.

Arroyo Grande High School and Beyond is an educational interlude.

Efron's formative years in theatre were intertwined with his studies. He graduated from Arroyo Grande High School in 2006, marking the end of one chapter and the beginning of another. His admittance to the University of Southern California demonstrated not just his academic ability but also his dedication to a comprehensive education in the performing arts.

However, Efron's career deviated from the usual collegiate route. Despite being accepted, he did not attend USC. Instead, he pursued a new path, enrolling in the Pacific Conservatory of the Performing Arts. This decision highlighted Efron's commitment to gaining hands-on experience in his chosen industry. The theatre company, based at Allan Hancock College, allowed Efron to continue honing his art in front of the demanding gaze of live audiences.

The story of Zac Efron's journey from the theatre to Hollywood is one of passion, perseverance, and the transformational power of live performance. The Great American Melodrama and Vaudeville, Gipsy, and other theatrical experiences developed him into an actor capable of switching between genres and mediums with ease.

Efron's early theatre origins not only established the framework for his Hollywood success, but also nurtured a real love for the profession of acting. The intimacy of the stage, the connection with the audience, and the demands of live performance all aided Efron's development as an actor capable of not just navigating the complexities of a screenplay but also captivating an audience with sincerity.

We unearth the vivid tapestry of Zac Efron's early years as we investigate his theatre roots. These chapters, sometimes buried by Hollywood's gloss, show a young artist developing his skills, embracing different roles, and laying the framework for a career that would transcend the limits of stage and cinema.

An Early Agent Connection

Zac Efron's foray into the glamorous world of Hollywood was marked by the marks of a fortuitous meeting that would determine the trajectory of his blossoming career. At the core of this watershed moment was Efron's high school acting instructor, Robyn Metchik, whose name would reverberate deeply throughout his career.

Robyn Metchik was more than just an educator in the quiet corridors of Arroyo Grande High School, where Efron spent his formative years. Her influence extended beyond the field of teaching dramatic arts to that pivotal moment when she recognised the potential emanating from her student, a talent that deserved a broader stage than the high school theatre.

Robyn Metchik's link to the entertainment industry was the impetus for Efron's move to Hollywood. A genuine acknowledgment of ability and a desire to see a talented young performer reach new heights, rather than a conventional business arrangement. Metchik, the mother of actor Aaron Michael Metchik, had her finger on the industry's pulse, and it was her astute eye that detected something special in Efron.

The recommendation to a Los Angeles agency was like handing Efron a golden ticket to the land where fantasies are weaved into the tapestry of reality. This act set in motion a chain of circumstances that would lead to auditions, callbacks, and, eventually, the doors of opportunity swinging wide open for the Arroyo Grande wannabe actor.

Connections are frequently the fulcrum that transforms potential into reality in the entertainment industry. Robyn Metchik's recommendation not only introduced Efron to Hollywood's convoluted ecosystem, but it also served as a testament to the importance of mentorship in the performing arts. It was a nod of affirmation from someone who had seen her student's spark of potential and trusted in his ability to shine on a far larger platform.

This early agency link was more than just a professional introduction; it was a bridge that connected Arroyo Grande's small-town charm to the glittering lights of Los Angeles. This relationship catapulted Efron's path from local theatre shows to the centre of the film industry, emphasising the necessity of mentorship and assistance in the stormy world of show business.

The symbiotic nature of such linkages in the entertainment business is worth mentioning. While Efron clearly profited from Metchik's recommendation, the subsequent chapters of his success story also demonstrated his own talent and perseverance. Hollywood can be a brutal environment, and simply getting a foot in the door does not guarantee permanence. Efron's following auditions, roles, and eventual breakthrough in High School Musical revealed that his early connection served as a springboard, but it was his talent and charisma that kept him flying.

This story about an early agency connection adds legitimacy to Efron's story. It debunks the notion of overnight success and emphasises the value of mentorship and direction, particularly in an industry notorious for its volatility. Robyn Metchik's participation in Efron's biography reminds us that there are often unsung heroes - mentors, teachers, or advisors - who recognise promise and help to the moulding of a spectacular career behind every celebrity.

In retrospect, recommending Efron to an agency was a watershed moment not only in his life, but also in the larger cultural scene. The ensuing chapters of his career, distinguished by iconic roles, box office success, and a varied spectrum of performances, can all be traced back to that initial nod of approval from a theatre teacher who spotted something special in a young actor.

It's a testament to the intertwined nature of the entertainment industry that we're delving into the details of Efron's early agency link. Hollywood, which is frequently seen as a large and impersonal entity, displays its human side via stories like these - scenarios in which personal relationships and mentorship play a crucial role in determining an artist's destiny.

To summarise, Zac Efron's path from Arroyo Grande to Hollywood is more than just a story of individual brilliance; it is also a story weaved with mentorship and serendipitous connections. The early agent link, made possible by Robyn Metchik's keen eye, was the beginning of a Hollywood journey that would see Efron become a household figure. It's a story about the symbiotic link between skill and opportunity, and it reminds us that in the complicated dance of show business, sometimes all it takes is one person who believes in your potential to set the scene for stardom.

Almost a Trojan

After graduating from Arroyo Grande High School in 2006, Zac Efron, the heartthrob of High School Musical, found himself at a crossroads. The stage was set for him to begin a new chapter at the esteemed University of Southern California, but fate had other intentions. This decision not to join represented a watershed moment in Efron's career, influencing the course of his career and providing insight into the complexity of selecting between conventional courses and the pull of stardom.

The Academic Road Less Travelled

While Efron excelled academically in high school, the allure of the performing arts drew him away from the sacred halls of traditional schooling. After being accepted to the University of Southern California, a bastion of academic brilliance, Efron found himself on the verge of a traditional undergraduate experience. The siren voice of Hollywood, with its promises of fame and money, however, rang louder in his ears.

A Pathway Divergence

The decision not to enroll at USC was not a rejection of education, but rather a deviation from the intended path. With a penchant for acting and a desire for the spotlight, Efron picked a different kind of classroom: Hollywood's studios and stages. It was a risk, a leap of faith into the unpredictability of the entertainment industry, where success is elusive and competition is strong.

The Allure of Fame

What made Efron decide to forsake the regular college experience? The answer is found in the seductive pull of celebrity. High School Musical had already cast its spell, catapulting Efron to stardom. The taste of triumph, fan adoration, and the potential of larger parts awaited him. The Hollywood ideal appeared to be within his grasp, and the limits of a university lecture hall couldn't match with the huge platform he imagined for himself.

A Worthwhile Risk

Choosing not to attend USC was essentially a calculated gamble. It was a choice to invest in his craft, to totally immerse himself in the world of acting without the safety net of a college degree. Efron's confidence in his abilities and the prospects that lied ahead fuelled this bold action. He had no idea that this risk would pay off with legendary roles, critical praise, and a lasting influence on popular culture.

Lessons Outside of the Classroom

While Efron did not pursue a traditional academic path, his career in the entertainment industry served as an unorthodox classroom. Every film set, every character played, was a lesson in the classroom of experience. The ups and downs of show business, the demanding nature of the profession, and the skill of reinvention were the lessons that fashioned him into more than simply a performer; they shaped him into a multifaceted actor capable of transcending his youthful idol image.

Act of Balance: Fame vs. Education

Efron's decision stirred discussions about the delicate balance between stardom and education. Is he missing out on the classic college experience? Perhaps. His on-the-job training in the brutally competitive world of Hollywood, however, provided a unique style of education not found in textbooks. While negotiating the complications of celebrity life, Efron, the persistent learner, absorbed the nuances of his profession.

Identity Impact: Actor vs. Student

The decision not to attend USC raised identification concerns. Would Efron be characterised solely by his on-screen roles, or might he have been a student pursuing academic excellence? This junction of personal and professional identity became a recurring motif in Efron's story, adding dimensions to the actor's public perception beyond the characters he portrayed.

Reflections and Hindsight

As the years passed, Efron's decision to forego traditional academics became a defining feature of his story. In retrospect, one might wonder about the "what ifs" of an alternative universe in which Efron swapped film sets for lecture halls. Nonetheless, his path, marked by highs, lows, and unexplored territory, demonstrates that the most exceptional stories are sometimes constructed outside the borders of convention.

The chapter in Zac Efron's life dubbed "Almost a Trojan" is still an important element of his biography. It exemplifies youth's daring, the appeal of dreams, and the determination to defy expectations. Efron's journey questions the conventional definition of success, emphasising that taking the road less travelled might lead to unexpected, yet profoundly satisfying, outcomes. As we turn the pages of his life, we discover that the unwritten chapters offer the possibility of even larger disclosures, indicating that his decision not to attend USC was, in fact, a prelude to a story that is still unfolding.

YouTube Account

In the ever-changing environment of celebrity involvement with their audience, Zac Efron made a huge leap into the digital sphere in March 2019 by starting his YouTube account. This was a significant step for the actor, as it gave viewers an intimate look into his life and interests through carefully curated content. Efron's YouTube channel provided a forum for him to share not only his adventures and outdoor escapades, but also his dedication to health and nutrition, displaying a varied element of his personality outside of the screen.

One of the main episodes on Efron's channel, titled "Off the Grid," offered a pleasant break from the glitz and glamour associated with Hollywood. This show became a doorway into Efron's exploration of outdoor hobbies and vacations, giving viewers an unvarnished peek at his adventures. In an increasingly technological world, "Off the Grid" featured an intentional effort to disconnect from electronic gadgets, with the exception of a video camera used to capture these trips. The series not only showcased Efron's adventurous spirit, but it also carried a deeper message about the value of reconnecting with nature in an increasingly digitised society.

The series title, "Off the Grid," reflects a purposeful desire to distance oneself from the regimented and frequently artificial surroundings of the entertainment industry. Efron and his brother Dylan embarked on adventures that included everything from hiking and camping to visiting distant locations. This series revealed a side of Efron that went beyond his on-screen character, demonstrating a true love of the outdoors and a devotion to living life outside of the restrictions of a studio or film set.

"Off the Grid" was complemented with another engrossing series called "Gym Time." This part changed the focus to Efron's commitment to fitness and nutrition, giving viewers a behind-the-scenes peek at his workout habits. The actor made it clear that the goal was not only to show off a glossy Hollywood workout; rather, "Gym Time" wanted to highlight the true effort and discipline required to live a healthy lifestyle. Efron stated his want to train alongside celebrities, sportsmen, and other interesting people, so establishing a venue where fitness fans and interested viewers alike may gain insight into his wellness journey.

The "Gym Time" series went into Efron's exercise routine, stressing not only the physical but also the mental and emotional sides of his health approach. The series created a forum for discussions about various fitness ideologies, dietary practices, and overall well-being by having a varied spectrum of guests. Efron's openness to reveal his personal fitness problems and accomplishments resulted in a relatable story that connected with people looking for inspiration for their own health and fitness journeys.

Efron made a conscious decision to embrace YouTube as a content-sharing platform. It enabled him to interact on a more personal level with a global audience, transcending the usual limitations of celebrity-fan relationships. Fans could interact directly with Efron's content via the platform, writing comments, sharing their own experiences, and experiencing a sense of kinship with the actor. Viewers were active participants in Efron's digital journey as a result of the two-way engagement.

Not only did Efron's YouTube channel garner attention for its content, but also for the platform's promotional techniques. The actor's decision to use his celebrity to generate digital material has sparked debate about the changing environment of internet platforms and their connection with popular entertainment. This move, however, was not without controversy. YouTube was chastised for promoting Efron's channel in an official Twitter post, with several users concerned that it will overshadow lesser-known producers. This incident emphasised the difficult balance that exists within the YouTube ecosystem between promoting big celebrity content and assisting emerging artists.

Efron's YouTube channel became a case study in the developing nature of celebrity involvement in the digital era, beyond the quantity of followers and views. It demonstrated the possibility for established performers to use platforms such as YouTube to tell stories that go beyond scripted parts and red carpet appearances. Efron's content approach was to inspire, entertain, and, at times, challenge society standards in the areas of technology, fitness, and outdoor adventures.

Finally, Zac Efron's foray into the world of YouTube was a watershed moment in his career. He drew viewers into his personal spaces through shows like "Off the Grid" and "Gym Time," exposing not only the glitz of Hollywood but also the rawness of outdoor experiences and the dedication required for a healthy lifestyle. Efron's YouTube account became a symbol of his adaptability and readiness to embrace new channels to communicate with his followers. It mirrored a broader trend in the entertainment industry, in which celebrities use digital platforms to construct their narratives, communicate with fans directly, and exhibit aspects of their personality that go beyond the written roles for which they are known. Zac Efron's YouTube channel was more than just a video collection; it was a digital diary, providing an authentic and uncensored peek into the life of a Hollywood celebrity navigating the realms of nature, fitness, and self-discovery.

Ascension to the Forbes Celebrity 100

Few awards carry the weight and grandeur of being named to the Forbes Celebrity 100 list in the ever-changing world of the entertainment industry, where celebrity often intertwines with money. For Zac Efron, the year 2008 was a watershed moment in his career, as he not only became a household celebrity but also ranked 92 on the prestigious list, demonstrating his stratospheric climb in the world of entertainment.

Forbes magazine's annual Forbes Celebrity 100 list acts as a barometer of a celebrity's influence and financial achievement. In Efron's case, his participation in the 2008 edition highlighted not only his popularity, but also the enormous riches he earned between June 2007 and June 2008. The estimated amount of $5.8 million indicated not only his status as a sought-after actor, but also the various routes through which he was monetizing his expanding renown.

Efron's rise to the Forbes Celebrity 100 list was the result of deliberate career decisions, hard effort, and an in-depth understanding of the entertainment industry. Efron was born on October 18, 1987, in San Luis Obispo, California, and his early years were distinguished by a love of performing, as seen by his participation in school theatre productions and singing training. However, it was his early 2000s television appearances in shows like Firefly, ER, and Summerland that paved the way for his rise.

The release of "High School Musical," a Disney Channel original film that quickly became a worldwide hit, in 2006 marked a watershed moment. Efron played Troy Bolton, a charming and musically inclined high school basketball star, a role that not only displayed his acting abilities but also launched him into the hearts of adolescent audiences worldwide. The enormous success of the film created the groundwork for a franchise, with Efron returning his part in subsequent movies, cementing his status as a teen idol.

As "High School Musical" grew in prominence, so did Efron's employment opportunities. Roles in films such as "Hairspray" (2007) and "17 Again" (2009) highlighted his crossover from television to the big screen, displaying his versatility outside the limits of the Disney Channel. These ventures not only broadened his target demographic, but also greatly contributed to his growing financial success.

However, it wasn't just acting that contributed to Efron's fortune. In 2010, he took a strategic step by launching Ninjas Runnin' Wild, his own production business under Warner Bros. This move highlighted Efron's entrepreneurial mentality, allowing him to participate in the creation of films such as "Dirty Grandpa," "That Awkward Moment," and "Extremely Wicked, Shockingly Evil and Vile." His broadening of his involvement in the industry provided another layer to his income stream, transforming him from a performer to a producer.

The release of "High School Musical 3: Senior Year" in 2008, the same year he made the Forbes Celebrity 100 list, marked another milestone in Efron's career. This installment brought the franchise to the big screen, solidifying its status as a box office smash. The success of the film not only increased Efron's salary but also demonstrated his ability to transition easily between television and film.

Efron's activities moved beyond acting and producing to endorsements and commercial collaborations. His image as a heartthrob and a symbol of youthful attractiveness made him a sought-after figure for numerous brands trying to break into the lucrative teenage market. Endorsement deals and partnerships expanded his financial portfolio, establishing him not only as an actor but also as a marketable personality.

The Forbes Celebrity 100 list is more than just a tally of profits; it also reflects a celebrity's cultural impact. In Efron's case, his inclusion on the list represented a shift in the landscape of celebrity, indicating that actors were more than just performers, but multifaceted personalities with the power to influence trends and consumer behaviour. His rise from "High School Musical" crooner to Forbes-listed celebrity spoke loudly about the changing dynamics of popularity in the twenty-first century.

It's worth noting that Efron's financial triumph was not without its difficulties and controversy. The scrutiny that comes with stardom, including aspects of his personal life and occasional public gaffes, complicated his journey. However, Efron's ability to negotiate the pitfalls of celebrity while constantly delivering performances that resonated with audiences demonstrated not only his talent but also his perseverance in the face of increased public scrutiny.

In retrospect, Efron's participation on the Forbes Celebrity 100 list captures a specific period in his career, encapsulating the convergence of talent, smart choices, and a quickly developing entertainment industry. The stated gains of $5.8 million are more than just a figure; they are a tribute to the entertainment industry's economic engine, where success is measured not only in praise but also in dollars and cents.

As the period covered by the Forbes Celebrity 100 list of 2008 came to an end, it was clear that Zac Efron had outgrown his early adolescent idol image. The world had watched the rise of an actor who, equipped with skill and economic acumen, had established himself as one of the entertainment industry's most important and financially successful personalities.

Health Challenges

Zac Efron's journey in the spotlight has not been easy, with unanticipated health difficulties testing his resilience and determination. One of the most notable events came in 2013, when Efron suffered a severe jaw injury, which proved to be a watershed moment in his life.

In the early months of 2013, Efron was dealing with a serious health problem that would not only impair his physical look but also have a negative impact on his general well-being. After a fall at home resulted in a fracture, the actor was forced to face the painful reality of having his jaw wired shut. This occurrence, which was initially thought to be a simple mishap, turned out to be a complex set of events that would have a tremendous impact on Efron's life.

It is never easy to decide to wire one's jaw shut. Aside from the physical discomfort and dietary changes, it confronted Efron with an unexpected hurdle. His capacity to communicate, which is critical to his job, was briefly hampered. This period of forced silence turned out to be a fascinating introspective journey for Efron, pushing him to reconsider different elements of his life and profession.

The true shock came years later, when Efron revealed the seriousness of the problem. In 2022, he openly admitted that the 2013 episode was a near-death experience rather than a transient time of adversity. The disclosure sent shockwaves across his fan base and the entertainment business, putting light on the seriousness of his health issues.

While the incident had been shrouded in secrecy for years, it was now revealed as a vital moment that tested Efron physically and intellectually. The actor's candour regarding the incident provided the world with insight into the emotional difficulties he faced behind the splendour of the red carpet. It humanizes a celebrity who is frequently viewed through the lens of celebrity, reminding us that no one is immune to health problems, regardless of fame or riches.

Efron's near-death experience caused him to ponder on the frailty of life and the significance of perseverance in the face of hardship. It became more than just a story about a fractured jaw; it became a story about survival, overcoming the unexpected, and emerging stronger on the other side.

The experience was also a watershed moment in Efron's connection with his own body. The actor, who is famed for his agility and physical power, was forced to confront vulnerability in ways he had never expected. However, when Efron accepted the process of healing, both physically and mentally, his vulnerability became a source of strength.

Beyond the physical problems, the incident's mental and emotional toll cannot be overstated. Efron, a performer who feeds on communication and expression, found himself in a brief period of stillness, forcing him to seek alternative forms of contact. During this time, he turned to transcendental meditation (TM) as a coping method, looking for solace and mental serenity in the midst of stress.

The discovery of Efron's near-fatal health problems triggered a broader discussion about the expectations and demands imposed on individuals in the entertainment industry. The public and media, which are notorious for scrutinising celebrities, were now presented with the hard fact that fame does not protect one from the unpredictability of life.

As Efron progressively recovered and returned to the public eye, his story acted as an inspiration to many who were dealing with health issues. His candour about the experience, including the ups and downs, aided in de-stigmatizing discussions about health and well-being. Efron emerged not only as a Hollywood hottie, but also as a courageous individual who faced mortality and emerged stronger.

Zac Efron's health issues, particularly the jaw injuries that nearly cost him his life, were a sad chapter in his life narrative. It emphasised the fragility of life, the unforeseen twists and turns it might take, and the resilience required to negotiate its difficulties. As Efron's career progresses, this chapter will stand as a testament to the actor's steadfast spirit and ability to discover growth in the most unexpected places.

Diet Alteration

One part in Zac Efron's ever-changing life story that sticks out prominently is his foray into daring diet alterations. The actor, known for his sculpted figure and dedication to a healthy lifestyle, took a daring step by committing to a vegan diet for an extended length of time before making a critical move in 2022. This transformation not only provoked discussions about his food choices, but it also shined light on the complex interplay between nutrition, well-being, and the demands of a successful Hollywood career.

Embracing Veganism: A Life-Changing Experience

Zac Efron's vegan journey was more than just a nutritional change; it signified a full lifestyle commitment. The choice to exclude animal products from his diet is consistent with the growing trend of celebrities adopting plant-based lifestyles for health, environmental, and ethical reasons. For two years, Efron lived a vegan lifestyle, making careful eating choices and experimenting with different protein sources.

The actor's vegetarianism extended beyond the dining table. His social media presence became a platform for promoting plant-based living, providing glimpses of colourful, plant-powered meals, and campaigning for environmentally friendly activities. Efron's impact extended beyond his fan group, leading to a broader public discussion on the benefits and drawbacks of living a vegan lifestyle.

A Paradigm Shift in Intermittent Fasting and the Return of Meat

However, as the year 2022 progressed, Efron began a new nutritional chapter, integrating intermittent fasting and reinstating meat into his diet. This was a significant shift, arousing curiosity and discussion regarding the actor's motivations. Intermittent fasting, defined by precise eating and fasting periods, is lauded for its possible health benefits, which include enhanced metabolism and weight management.

The reintroduction of meat into Efron's diet coincided with information about food sensitivity tests. The actor's willingness to disclose this piece of his personal health struggle adds legitimacy to his story. While not without controversy, food sensitivity testing is an emerging trend in personalized nutrition, attempting to discover foods that may cause adverse reactions in individuals. Efron's candour about the procedure adds to the continuing debate about the junction of science, health, and dietary choices.

Navigating the Dietary Landscape: Obstacles and Successes

Efron's transition from veganism to a more flexible nutritional strategy begs reflection on the challenges and successes that such big changes entail. Veganism, with its ethical and environmental concerns, may be a rewarding but challenging lifestyle choice. The actor's decision to consume meat reflects a pragmatic recognition of the complexities of individual nutritional needs and the developing understanding of dietary science.

The public debate around Efron's nutritional journey reflects a broader cultural debate regarding the influence of celebrity choices on lifestyle trends. The actor's ability to navigate this terrain with transparency assists to the breakdown of strict dietary conceptions. It expresses a recognition that food choices are fluid, impacted by personal experiences, health considerations, and developing scientific knowledge.

Beyond the Plate: Zac Efron's Holistic Approach to Health

Zac Efron's foray into daring dietary modifications goes beyond ordinary gastronomic preferences. It reveals a holistic approach to well-being that includes physical health, mental resilience, and adaptability. The actor's candour regarding his battles with insomnia, agoraphobia, and depression emphasises the importance of lifestyle choices in mental health.

The adoption of intermittent fasting into Efron's regimen not only demonstrates his versatility, but also appeals with a broader audience looking for sustainable and science-backed strategies for health optimisation. His experience highlights the value of a holistic and individualised approach to wellbeing, recognising that there is no one-size-fits-all solution.

Cultural Influence and Celebrity Influence

Celebrity diets are frequently used as cultural touchstones, influencing trends and moulding ideas of health and fitness. Efron's nutritional change is a case study in how popular figures can influence nutrition conversations.

The actor illustrates the fluidity of dietary choices and the need of listening to one's body, from being a prominent champion for veganism to accepting a more flexible approach.

The combination of celebrity influence and food choices raises concerns about the accountability that comes with stardom. Efron's openness to discuss the highs and lows of his nutritional journey contributes to a more nuanced understanding of the problems people confront when making dietary adjustments, refuting the myth that there is a perfect, one-size-fits-all approach to wellbeing.

The unifying theme in Zac Efron's gastronomic voyage is adaptation, from adopting vegetarianism to reintroducing intermittent fasting and meat into his diet. His path transcends dietary labels, reminding us that well-being is a dynamic, ever-changing process. In the face of public scrutiny, Efron's story becomes a tapestry woven with threads of personal choice, health consciousness, and a devotion to authenticity.

As the actor navigates the spotlight, his food choices offer a window into the larger social discourse about health, individualism, and the impact of celebrity influence. In a world where fad diets sometimes dominate headlines, Efron's story provides a new take on the significance of listening to one's body and taking a holistic approach to well-being. Far from being static, the culinary chapters of his life unfold as a tribute to the continual examination of what it means to live a healthy and full life in public.

Philanthropy and Environmental Causes

Zac Efron's influence extends far beyond Hollywood's glitz and glamour, as he is deeply involved in philanthropy and environmental causes, demonstrating a desire to make a positive difference in the world. This chapter goes into the different activities and programmes that demonstrate Efron's commitment to making a difference, highlighting the actor's philanthropic side and his efforts to improve society and the earth.

Zac Efron's involvement with charitable organisations committed to various causes is an important aspect of his philanthropic path. Efron recognised the necessity of using his position to address social concerns and effect genuine change early in his career. His philanthropy initiatives are extensive, reflecting his diverse interests and the depth of his commitment to making a positive influence.

Efron has been an advocate for a number of humanitarian organisations, using his celebrity to generate awareness and support for causes near and dear to his heart. Whether it's efforts relating to education, healthcare, or social justice, Efron has continually used his celebrity to bring attention to important topics. Beyond simply signing a cheque, Efron actively participates in events, initiatives, and outreach programmes, exhibiting a hands-on commitment to making a difference.

Environmental protection is one major concern that Efron has actively supported. The actor has been vocal about his environmental concerns and has taken tangible actions to help save our planet. Efron's involvement in projects designed at raising awareness about climate change, supporting sustainable practices, and campaigning for the conservation of endangered species exemplifies his dedication to environmental causes.

One of Efron's major contributions to environmental conservation is his appearance in the Netflix series "Down to Earth with Zac Efron." This travel documentary not only highlights Efron's adventurous attitude, but it also provides a platform for global exploration of sustainable living techniques. Efron interacts with experts, local groups, and environmentalists in the series, boosting their voices and teaching viewers on the significance of adopting eco-friendly lives.

Aside from his efforts on-screen, Efron has taken steps in his personal life to line with his environmental principles. His decision to transfer to Australia in 2021 was driven not just by his commitment to living in harmony with nature, but also by his desire to live in harmony with nature. With its numerous ecosystems and emphasis on environmental conservation, Australia allows Efron to immerse himself in a community that shares his ideals.

Furthermore, Efron's commitment to environmental problems goes beyond the entertainment sector. The actor has actively supported environmental organisations, lending his voice to campaigns addressing topics such as deforestation, plastic pollution, and climate change. Efron amplifies these important ideas by leveraging his stardom, reaching a larger audience and inspiring collective action.

Efron's commitment in environmental matters extends beyond awareness campaigns; he has also invested in ventures that directly benefit conservation efforts. Whether it's donating to wildlife sanctuaries, funding forestry projects, or cooperating with organisations dedicated to sustainable development, Efron's charitable efforts strive to produce tangible, beneficial results for the environment.

Aside from environmental causes, Efron has been actively interested in healthcare and well-being programmes. His philanthropic donations to organisations targeting medical research, illness prevention, and mental health represent a multifaceted approach to giving. Efron understands the interconnectivity of numerous societal concerns and aspires to have a significant effect on multiple fronts.

Finally, Zac Efron's humanitarian career demonstrates his dedication to making a positive difference in the world. His commitment in a wide range of topics, from environmental protection to healthcare, demonstrates a genuine desire to help society. Efron goes above the position of a celebrity by leveraging his influence, platform, and personal resources to become a catalyst for change and a beacon of inspiration for others to join in the pursuit of a better, more sustainable society.

Bacterial Infection in Papua New Guinea.

Few stories in the annals of celebrity escapades have the gravity and tenacity demonstrated by Zac Efron during his terrifying experience with a deadly bacterial infection in Papua New Guinea. This occurrence occurred in December 2019, marking a watershed moment in Efron's life that highlighted not only the hazards involved with exploration, but also the character required to face unexpected challenges.

The Unveiling of "Killing Zac Efron": A Daring Expedition

At the centre of this story is Efron's ambitious project, the documentary series "Killing Zac Efron." The series, conceived as an investigation of Papua New Guinea's untamed landscapes, promised an unedited peek into the actor's adventure as he navigated the bush, challenging his survival skills in a raw and brutal setting. Efron had no idea that this journey would turn into a life-changing battle against a terrible foe—bacterial illness.

The Mysterious Papua New Guinea: A Setting for Adversity

With its deep rainforests and rough terrain, Papua New Guinea provided a tough background for Efron's expedition. The tropical appeal of this island nation belied the underlying dangers that would soon await Efron as the cameras rolled and he ventured into the heart of the unknown. The very scenery that lured with its beauty would prove to be a test of Efron's fortitude.

A Fatal Encounter: The Beginning of Infection

Efron's adventure took an unexpected turn in the lush expanses of Papua New Guinea. During the course of his adventure, the actor encountered a terrible foe: a nasty bacterial infection. The nature of the sickness, which was defined as a "form of typhoid or similar bacterial infection," put a shadow over Efron's trip, changing what was supposed to be a triumph of survival into a struggle for life itself.

Medical Emergency: Airlifted to St. Andrews War Memorial Hospital

The urgency of Efron's situation demanded immediate and urgent action. He was transported to St. Andrews War Memorial Hospital in Brisbane, Australia, in December 2019, a journey that highlighted the gravity of the situation. The hospital became the battleground where Efron would combat the risks of the infection that had taken root in his system as the world awaited updates on the actor's condition.

Recovery: A Difficult Return to Health

The path to recovery was difficult for Zac Efron. The actor, known for his physical strength and on-screen magnetism, suddenly confronted an internal foe. Despite this, Efron maintained the same tenacity that had propelled him to the top of the entertainment world. According to reports, he recovered quickly, a monument to both his fortitude and the medical intervention that brought him back from the brink.

Post-Infection Reflections: A Different Point of View

The actor's battle with a severe bacterial infection in Papua New Guinea left an unforgettable impression on him. The near-death experience with a potentially fatal sickness sparked significant thoughts about mortality, perseverance, and the unpredictability of life's courses. It wasn't just a physical recovery; it was a mental transformation—a rebalancing of priorities and a fresh understanding for the frailty of human existence.

The Impact Beyond the Personal: A Lesson for Everyone

As word spread about Efron's health problem, it became more than just a personal story. It grew into a shared lesson in perseverance and the unpredictability of life's trials. Many people respected Efron not only for his on-screen charisma but also for his resilience in the face of hardship, thanks to his honesty about his health difficulties.

Efron's Unyielding Spirit: A Legacy of Resilience

Following this harrowing journey, Zac Efron emerged not just as a Hollywood heartthrob, but also as a symbol of unshakable determination. His journey from the brink of death to a victorious recovery became a tribute to the human potential to confront adversity, conquer it, and emerge stronger on the other side. Efron's story went beyond the realms of entertainment, serving as a light of hope for those facing similar challenges.

Zac Efron's experience with a dangerous bacterial infection in Papua New Guinea goes beyond the scope of a celebrity story. It's a narrative about vulnerability, resilience, and the unpredictability of life's adventures. Efron faced a test that went beyond survival skills in the middle of the deep rainforests, where danger waited around every corner. It was a test of the human spirit. His victorious return from the brink of death serves as a reminder that, in the face of adversity, the tenacious will to live triumphs, leaving an indelible impression on the actor's life and legacy.

The Future

Zac Efron finds himself at a crossroads in the ever-changing environment of Hollywood, his career distinguished by a varied assortment of roles that have shown his ability as an actor. As we dive into Efron's future ideas and ambitions, it becomes clear that he is not willing to rest on his past triumphs, but is motivated by an insatiable thirst for new challenges and creative discovery.

Future Projects: A Look at Efron's Creative Canvas

Zac Efron's career canvas continues to grow, with a slew of future projects that promise to further define his artistic individuality. "The Iron Claw," a film that delves into the world of wrestling and uncovers the intriguing story of the Von Erich family, is one of the most anticipated releases. Efron's portrayal of Kevin Von Erich carries the possibility of unravelling a character deeply ingrained in wrestling history, demonstrating his dedication to parts that defy expectations.

In addition to wrestling drama, Efron has dabbled in a variety of genres, demonstrating a willingness to broaden his storytelling horizons. "Gold," directed by Anthony Hayes, is a departure from his prior roles, thrusting him into a high-stakes story where the line between survival and surrender blurs. At the same time, the horror genre beckons with "Firestarter," an adaptation of Stephen King's classic in which Efron plays a character terrorised by otherworldly forces. These picks not only demonstrate Efron's versatility, but also his preference for stories that challenge the status quo.

However, Efron's passion extends beyond the silver screen. The actor has dabbled in digital content creation, utilising his production firm, Ninjas Runnin' Wild, to create content that transcends traditional channels. Efron's ability to adapt to the changing landscape of the entertainment industry is exemplified by the mix of traditional filming with digital storytelling.

Aims Outside of the Spotlight

While his professional history is shaped by his filmography, Zac Efron's ambitions transcend beyond the spotlight. His foray into production with Ninjas Runnin' Wild indicates not only a desire for creative freedom, but also puts him as an important participant in generating storylines that appeal with audiences. Efron's decision to create films such as "Dirty Grandpa," "That Awkward Moment," and "Extremely Wicked, Shockingly Evil and Vile" demonstrates his dedication to projects that transcend genre rules and question society prejudices.

Efron's foray into the digital arena via his YouTube account is also important. The "Off the Grid" and "Gym Time" programmes not only provide an insight into his personal life, but also allow him to engage with fans directly. In a world characterised by rapid celebrity access, Efron's entry into the digital landscape demonstrates a willingness to share actual experiences and communicate with fans in ways that go beyond traditional media's scripted tales.

Efron's dedication to health and wellbeing, as exemplified by the "Gym Time" series, represents a genuine desire to inspire positive living choices. In a world where celebrity influence frequently extends to lifestyle trends, Efron's decision to focus on fitness and nutrition becomes a statement about leveraging his platform to promote holistic well-being.

Entertainment Industry Legacies

It's impossible to deny Zac Efron's profound influence on popular culture as we consider his legacy in the entertainment world. From the soaring popularity of 'High School Musical' to nuanced performances in films such as 'The Greatest Showman' and 'Extremely Wicked, Shockingly Evil and Vile', Efron has walked a fine line between commercial appeal and critical acclaim.

His reputation includes a willingness to take risks and embrace roles that challenge cultural standards, in addition to box office statistics and honours. The transition from "High School Musical" teen heartthrob to the nuanced characters of Ted Bundy and Kevin Von Erich represents a purposeful decision to eschew typecasting and pursue parts that add to the larger tapestry of storytelling.

Furthermore, Efron's candour about personal hardships, such as substance misuse and mental health issues, lends credibility to his legacy. In a field that is frequently wrapped in glamour, his willingness to disclose his flaws humanises him and resonates with people dealing with similar issues.

Looking ahead, Zac Efron's legacy appears to be defined not only by the characters he portrays on screen, but also by the narratives he chooses to support and the influence he has on the industry. Efron emerges as a multifaceted artist whose legacy exceeds the constraints of a standard Hollywood narrative, whether through new internet material, diversified film roles, or a commitment to holistic well-being.

Finally, Chapter Thirteen provides a glimpse into Zac Efron's future career—a future defined by creative audacity, a commitment to varied storytelling, and a legacy that stretches beyond the glitz of the red carpet. As the curtain rises on the next chapter of his journey, Efron's trajectory continues to captivate audiences, leaving them anxious to see the unfolding chapters of a career that defies prediction and embraces the limitless possibilities of the cinematic canvas.

The Man Beyond the Celebrity

As we near the end of this Zac Efron biography, it becomes clear that his life is more than simply the flash and glamour of Hollywood. We've delved into the many dimensions of his life via the pages of this book, from the scenic vistas of Arroyo Grande to the hectic streets of Hollywood, and now to the tranquil coastlines of Australia.

Thoughts on Zac Efron's Incredible Journey

Zac Efron's path has been exceptional in every way. It's a story that will speak to anybody seeking encouragement in the face of adversity, not just his fervent supporters. His journey from a theater-loving child in California to an international sensation is a monument to his tenacity, talent, and unwavering dedication to the industry.

The success of High School Musical was a watershed moment in Efron's career, catapulting him to prominence. The post-Troy Bolton path, on the other hand, revealed a performer anxious to break free from the limits of an adolescent heartthrob image. From dramatic parts in films such as "Me and Orson Welles" to portraying real-life figures such as Ted Bundy in "Extremely Wicked, Shockingly Evil and Vile," Efron demonstrated his versatility and dedication to his craft.

Zac Efron's entrepreneurial side is also evident in his development of Ninjas Runnin' Wild, a production firm that played an important role in bringing his creative concepts to life. He also dabbled in presenting, receiving a Daytime Emmy for "Down to Earth with Zac Efron." This shift from actor to content creator demonstrates his versatility in an ever-changing entertainment world.

Efron's move to Australia is more than just a change of scenery; it represents a personal and professional transformation. The decision to immerse himself in a foreign culture and take on projects in a new setting demonstrates his daring spirit and desire to welcome change.

The Man Behind the Star

The investigation of Zac Efron, the guy beyond the star, is what genuinely distinguishes this book. Behind the red carpet appearances and blockbuster hits is a person who has overcome personal challenges. The revelations about his struggles with alcoholism, substance addiction, and mental health difficulties provide an uncensored look at the man behind the icon.

Efron's candour about his difficulties, especially the jaw injury that almost killed him, serves as a powerful reminder of the frailty of even the most seemingly invincible figures. His road to rehabilitation, sobriety, and a newfound commitment to health is a story of victory over adversity, with universal resonance.

The decision to incorporate transcendental meditation into his life, especially after portraying such a horrible figure as Ted Bundy, adds a depth of contemplation. It depicts a man who is aware of the toll his art may have on the mind and takes proactive steps to maintain mental health.

His foray into producing digital material, as well as the creation of a YouTube channel with programmes highlighting outdoor experiences and fitness activities, humanises the celebrity even further. It's a purposeful attempt to engage with the public beyond the planned parts and red carpet events, revealing the person behind the persona.

Zac Efron's involvement with charities, environmental causes, and his transition into a more conscientious lifestyle, including a stint of veganism, demonstrates his desire to make a positive influence outside of the entertainment industry. It's a side of his personality that is frequently overshadowed by the bright veneer of Hollywood, but it's crucial to know the man who lives when the cameras are turned off.

With Anticipation

As we come to the end of our journey through Zac Efron's life, the finale serves as a portal to the future. Efron's future endeavours, whether in cinema, production, or personal hobbies, promise to be a constant source of growth and reinvention.

His legacy is more than a collection of cinematic triumphs; it is a monument to the strength of character and the capacity for reinvention. Zac Efron, the man beyond the star, urges us to reflect not only on his journey, but also on our own journeys of self-discovery, perseverance, and honesty.

We bid farewell to the pages that have unfurled the chapters of Zac Efron's life as we conclude this biography. However, when the book comes to a close, the echoes of his trip linger—a voyage that extends beyond the limelight and exposes a man who, like all of us, navigates the complexity of life, always growing and leaving an unforgettable impression on the world.

Made in the USA
Columbia, SC
07 January 2024